A Germ's Journey

by Thom Rooke, MD

illustrated by Tony Trimmer

PICTURE WINDOW BOOKS
a capstone imprint

Special thanks to our adviser, Terry Flaherty, PhD, Professor of English, Minnesota State University, Mankato, for his expertise.

Editor: Jill Kalz
Designer: Tracy Davies
Art Director: Nathan Gassman
Production Specialist: Sarah Bennett
The illustrations in this book were created with mixed media/found object.

Picture Window Books
151 Good Counsel Drive
P.O. Box 669
Mankato, MN 56002-0669
877-845-8392
www.capstonepub.com

 All books published by Picture Window Books are manufactured with paper containing at least 10 percent post-consumer waste.

Library of Congress Cataloging-in-Publication Data
Rooke, Thom W.
  A germ's journey / by Thom Rooke, M.D. ; illustrated by Tony Trimmer.
    p. cm. — (Follow it!)
  Includes index.
  ISBN 978-1-4048-6268-5 (library binding)
  ISBN 978-1-4048-6710-9 (paperback)
  1. Germs—Juvenile literature. 2. Cold (Disease)—Juvenile literature. I. Trimmer, Tony. II. Title.
  QR57.R66 2011
  616.2'05—dc22   2010033765

Printed in the United States of America in North Mankato, Minnesota.
092010
005933CGS11

This is Rudy. Rudy feels rotten.
He has a cold.

Colds are caused by tiny creatures
called germs.

And right now, millions of germs
are living inside Rudy's nose.

Many types of germs can make
you sick. Examples include bacteria, mold,
fungi, and viruses. Colds are usually caused
by viruses called rhinoviruses.

3

The cold germs inside Rudy's nose are multiplying. They're running out of room and need a new home. Another nice, warm nose would be perfect!

The germs tickle Rudy's nose and trigger a ...

Excuse me!

Let's blow out of this place!

hello!

In real life, germs are very small. They can't be seen without a microscope.

5

SNEEZE!

Rudy forgot to use a tissue. His cold germs fly across the room at more than 100 miles an hour.

A few germs land on Ernie. But skin acts like a suit of armor. It protects against harm. The germs won't find a new home there.

Healthy skin keeps germs out. But germs can sneak into the body through cuts, scrapes, or cracks in the skin. Most germs enter through a person's mouth or nose.

Rudy's germs continue to fall on nearly everything in the room—including Brenda's candy.

Brenda can't see the germs. And she's hungry! Are the germs going to make her sick?

I think we found a new place to party!

Not today!

Brenda peels off the wrapper and throws it away. The germs wind up in the trash, not in her mouth.

Was it something we said?

Germs that land on floors, desks, or tissues usually dry up quickly and die. But some germs can live on objects for several days.

Eve is going to give an apple to her teacher.
Apples are supposed to be healthy snacks.
But this one might make Eve's teacher sick.

Wait!

Eve's teacher washes her apple before she eats it. The germs roll off and swirl down the drain.

Soap kills germs. So do hand sanitizers and antiseptics such as rubbing alcohol. Hand washing is the best way to keep germs from spreading.

11

Some of Rudy's germs land on the classroom computer. When Chip touches the keyboard, the germs stick to his fingers.

Chip didn't wash his hands after using the computer. He touches the doorknob. The pencil sharpener. His homework. He even touches the globe. Now *France* is contaminated with germs!

Oh, no!

Ooh, la la!

13

Yikes!

Here comes Jared. He types at the keyboard Chip just used. The germs are on the move again.

There are 400 times more germs on desktops and computer keyboards than there are on most toilet seats.

14

Jared rubs his eyes.
(That's bad.)

He bites his fingernails.
(That's worse.)

And now he ...
picks his nose.

Rudy's cold germs are now inside Jared's nose.
They multiply—quickly.

Soon the millions of germs will run out of room. They will spread to Jared's throat and lungs, and Jared will have a terrible cold.

Jared doesn't *feel* really sick—yet. But he can still spread germs, especially if he doesn't cover his mouth.

The germs find new homes, miles from school. And they don't stop there. They travel to dance class, piano lessons, and baseball games. They travel to restaurants and birthday parties—even to the movies!

Tonight, Jared finds out he is leaving this weekend to visit his grandmother—in Ohio.

The germs that started with Rudy are off on a brand-new adventure!

There is no cure for a common cold. Cold germs will disappear on their own, usually in a week or two.

Germ Journey Diagram

Glossary

antiseptic—a chemical that is used to kill certain germs outside a person's body

contaminate—to take something clean and get dirt, germs, or other bad things on it

multiply—to make more of something

rhinovirus—a type of virus that causes a cold

sanitizer—a cleaning liquid, gel, or other substance that gets rid of germs

To Learn More

More Books to Read

Cobb, Vicki. *Your Body Battles a Cold.* Body Battles. Minneapolis: Millbrook Press, 2009.

Goodbody, Slim. *Staying Well.* Slim Goodbody's Good Health Guides. Milwaukee: Gareth Stevens Pub., 2007.

Larsen, C. S. *Crust & Spray: Gross Stuff in Your Eyes, Ears, Nose, and Throat.* Gross Body Science. Minneapolis: Millbrook Press, 2010.

Internet Sites

FactHound offers a safe, fun way to find Internet sites related to this book. All of the sites on FactHound have been researched by our staff.

Here's all you do:
Visit *www.facthound.com*
Type in this code: 9781404862685

Check out projects, games and lots more at
www.capstonekids.com

Index

coughing, 19
cures, 21
entry into body, 7, 15, 19
hand washing, 11, 13
killing germs, 11
lifespan of germs, 9, 21
lungs, 17
mouth, 7, 9, 18, 19
nose, 3, 4, 5, 7, 15, 16

numbers of germs, 14
size of germs, 5
skin, 7
sneezing, 6
soap, 11
throat, 17
tissues, 6, 9
types of germs, 3
viruses, 3

Look for all the books in the Follow It series:

A Dollar Bill's Journey
A Germ's Journey

A Plastic Bottle's Journey
A Raindrop's Journey